PIANO / VOCAL / GUITAR

Dr. John

SHEET MUSIC ANTHOLOGY

Cover photo © Getty Images / Andy Sheppard / Contributor

ISBN 978-1-5400-2747-4

Visit Hal Leonard Online at
www.halleonard.com

Contact Us:
Hal Leonard
7777 West Bluemound Road
Milwaukee, WI 53213
Email: info@halleonard.com

In Europe contact:
Hal Leonard Europe Limited
42 Wigmore Street
Marylebone, London, W1U 2RN
Email: info@halleonardeurope.comm

In Australia contact:
Hal Leonard Australia Pty. Ltd.
4 Lentara Court
Cheltenham, Victoria, 3192 Australia
Email: info@halleonard.com.au

BRING YOUR OWN ALONG

Words and Music by
MAC REBENNACK

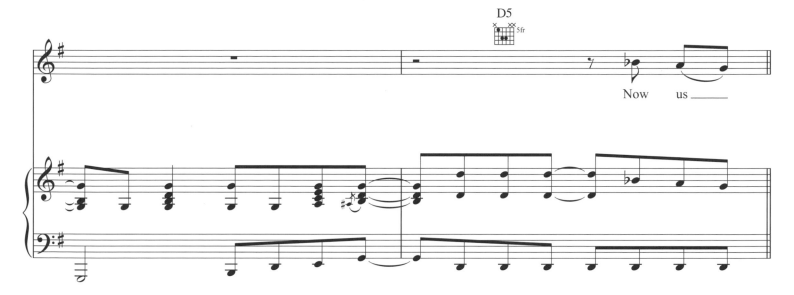

Now us ———

Ca - jun folks is poor. ——— We sell ———
Ca - jun folks is poor. ——— We sell ———
Ca - jun folks is poor. ——— Trap ———

musk - rat and sell their skin. ———
musk - rat and sell their skin. ———
musk - rats and sell their skin. ———

own a - long. _____ Ev - er - y - bod - y bring your
own a - long. _____ Ev - er - y - bod - y bring your

To Coda ⊕

own a - long. We're gon - na have us a craw - fish soi - rée,
own a - long. We're gon - na have us a craw - fish soi - rée,
(3.) *(Solo ends)*

sing some Ca - jun song. ___ ha'ing a ___ craw - fish soi -
sing some Ca - jun song. ___ have us a craw - fish soi -

- rée. Ev - er - y - bod - y bring your
- rée. Ev - er - y - bod - y bring your

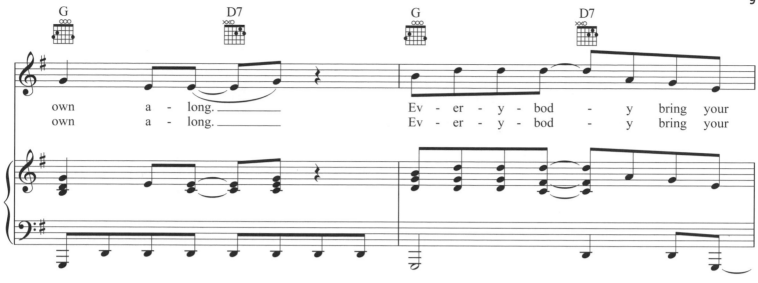

own a - long. _____ Ev - er - y - bod - y bring your
own a - long. _____ Ev - er - y - bod - y bring your

own a long. _ Feed Hec - tor Was - low.
own a - long. _ (2.) *Piano solo ad lib.*

Brought me a hat to cool me on. ___ Flop - py Hec - tor Was -

- low. _____ Ev - er - y - bod - y bring your own a - long. _____

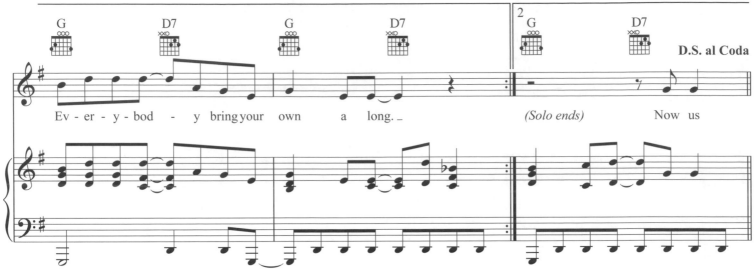

D.S. al Coda

Ev - er - y - bod - y bring your own a long. _____ *(Solo ends)* Now us

Down yon - der rev - el - ry,

old horn sounds good to me. _____ Me and _____ my sweet _____

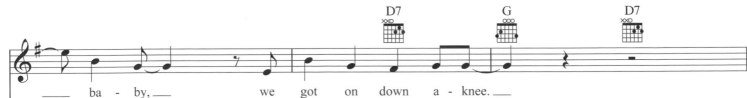

_____ ba - by, _____ we got on down a - knee. _____

Harmonica solo ad lib.

Repeat and Fade

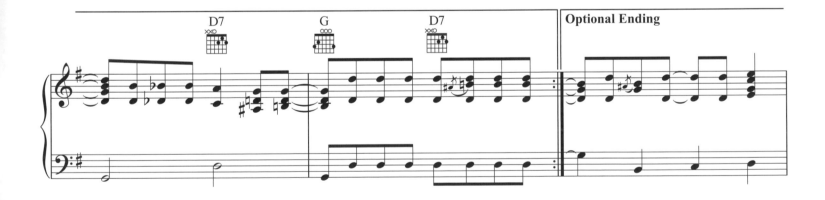

Optional Ending

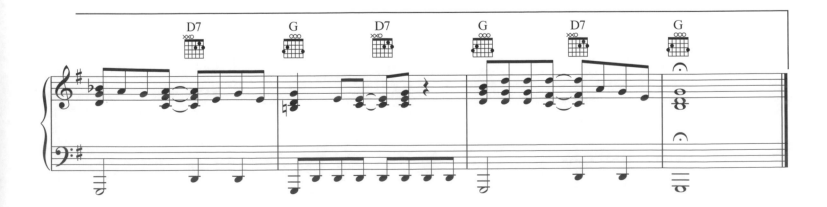

(Everybody Wanna Get Rich)
RITE AWAY

Words and Music by
MAC REBENNACK

Moderate Funk groove

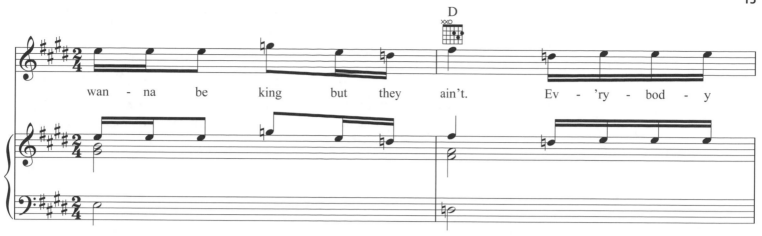

wan - na be king but they ain't. Ev - 'ry - bod - y

wan - na get rich right a - way. Wan - na be rich, say you wan - na be wealth - y. Be -

lieve I'd rath - er be poor __ and health - y. Wan - na be rich, say you wan - na be wealth - y. Be -

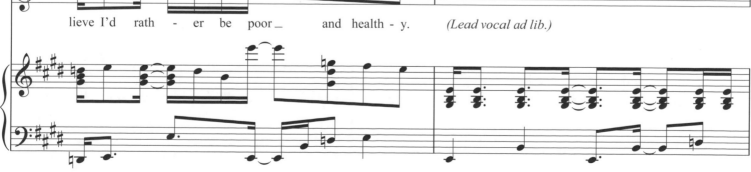

lieve I'd rath - er be poor __ and health - y. *(Lead vocal ad lib.)*

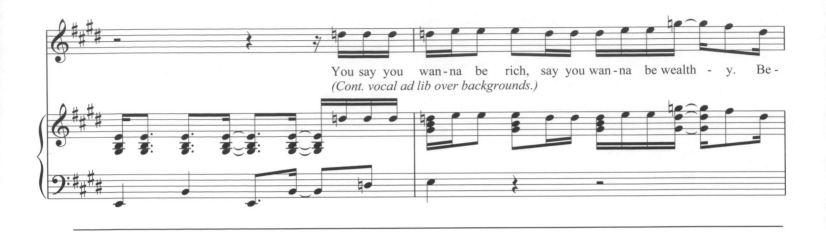

You say you wan-na be rich, say you wan-na be wealth - y. Be-
(Cont. vocal ad lib over backgrounds.)

lieve I'd rath - er be poor __ and health - y. Wan-na be rich, say you wan-na be wealth - y. Be-

lieve I'd rath - er be poor __ and health - y. Wan-na be rich, say you wan-na be wealth - y. Be-

lieve I'd rath - er be poor __ and health - y. Wan-na be rich, say you wan-na be wealth - y. Be-
And ev - *(Lead vocal ad lib. over backgrounds.)*

lieve I'd rath - er be poor _ and health - y. Spend fast as you can make _ it. You know that there's

Repeat and Fade

some - bod - y wait-in' to take _ it. You say you wan-na be rich, say you wan-na be wealth - y. Be-
(Cont. vocal ad lib over backgrounds.)

lieve I'd rath - er be poor _ and health - y. Wan-na be rich.

Optional Ending

You say you wan - na be rich.

DOWN IN NEW ORLEANS

from THE PRINCESS AND THE FROG

Music and Lyrics by
RANDY NEWMAN

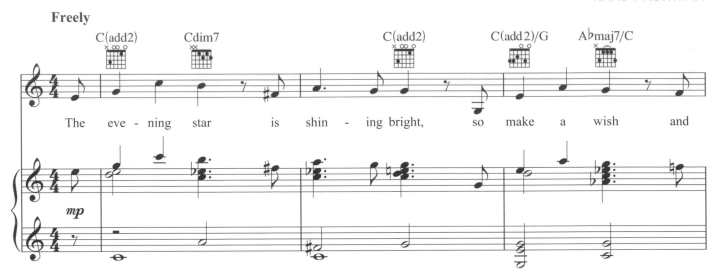

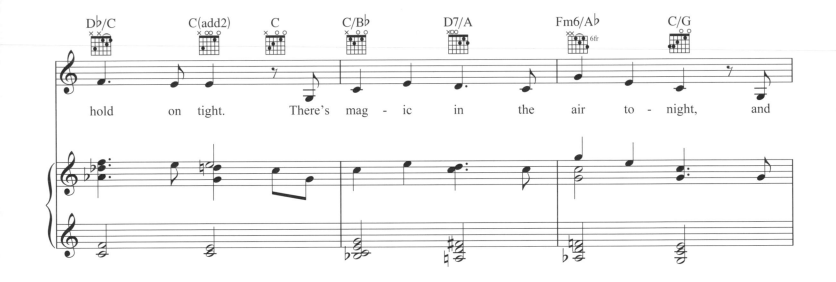

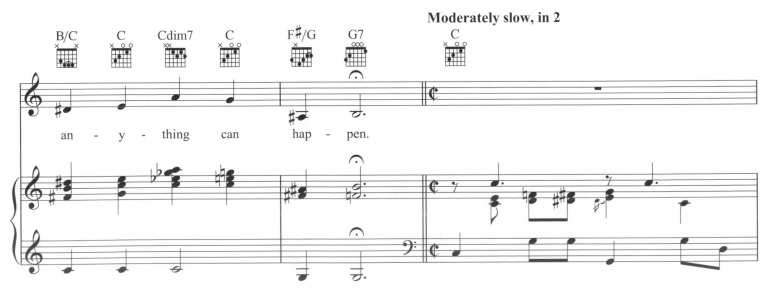

In the South - land there's a cit - y

way down _____ on the riv - er, _____ where the wom - en are ver -

y pret - ty and all the men de - liv - er. __

They got mu - sic, it's al - ways play - ing,
We got mag - ic, good and __ bad, __

start in the day - time, go all through the night. __
make __ you hap - py or make you real sad. __

When you hear __ that mu - sic play - ing,
Get ev - 'ry - thing you want, __ lose what you had,

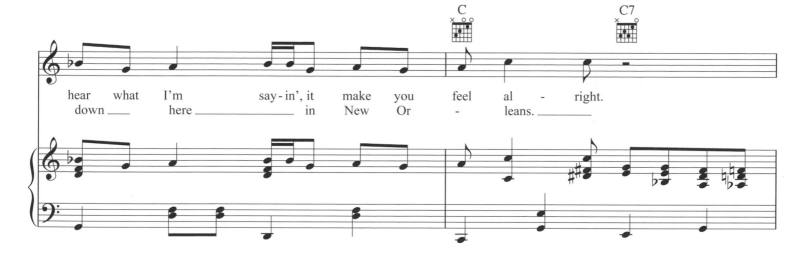

hear what I'm say-in', it make you feel al - right.
down ___ here ___ in New Or - leans. ___

Grab some-bod - y, come on ___ down. ___
Hey ___ part - ner, don't be ___ shy; ___

Bring your paint - brush; we're paint - in' the town. ___
come on down ___ here and give us a try. ___ You

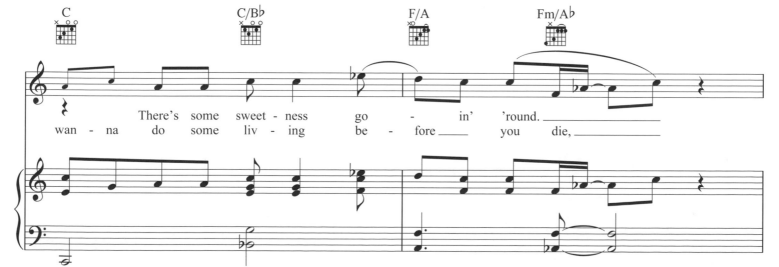

There's some sweet - ness go - in' 'round. ___
wan - na do some liv - ing be - fore ___ you die, ___

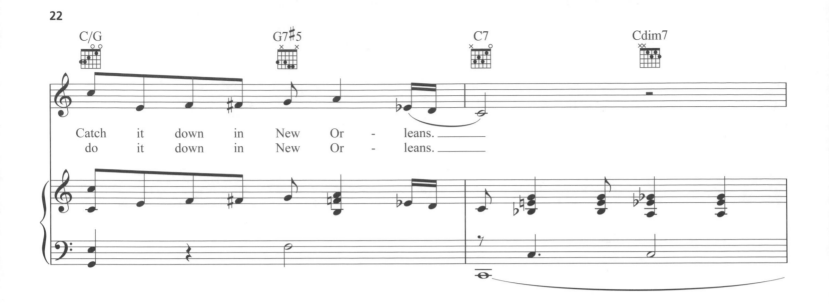

Catch it down in New Or - leans. _____
do it down in New Or - leans. _____

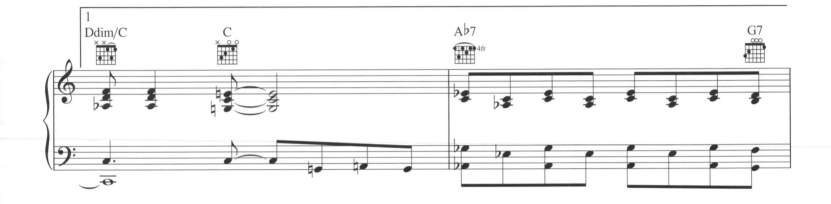

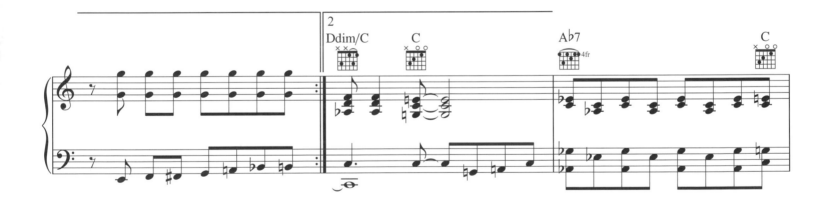

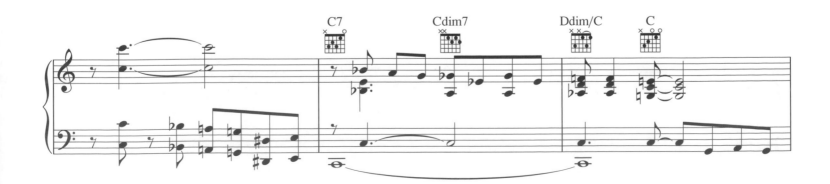

GOING BACK TO NEW ORLEANS

Words and Music by
JOSEPH LIGGINS

Moderate Mambo

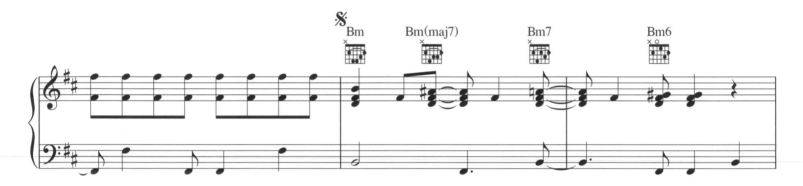

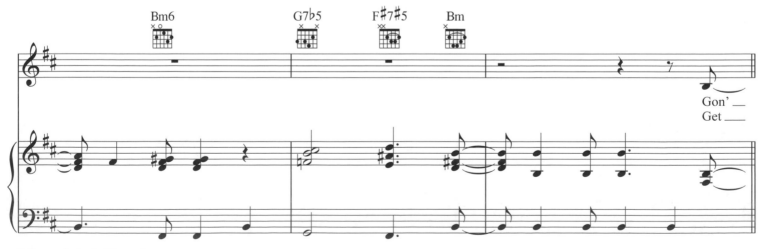

Gon' ___
Get ___

Recorded a half step lower.

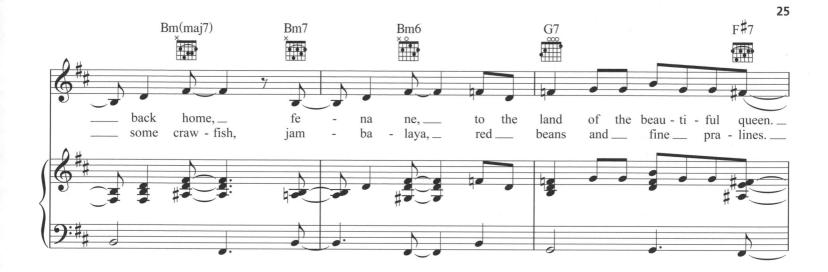

back home, __ fe - na ne, __ to the land of the beau - ti - ful queen. __
some craw - fish, jam - ba - laya, __ red __ beans and __ fine pra - lines. __

Gon' __ back home __ to my __ ba - by, __ go - in'
Get __ some lov - in' that gon' __ sat - is - fy __

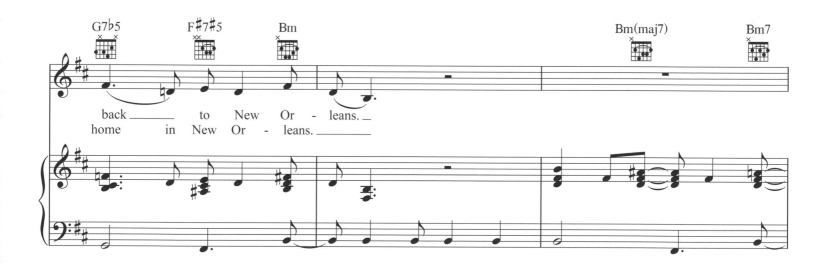

back __ to New Or - leans. __
home in New Or - leans. __

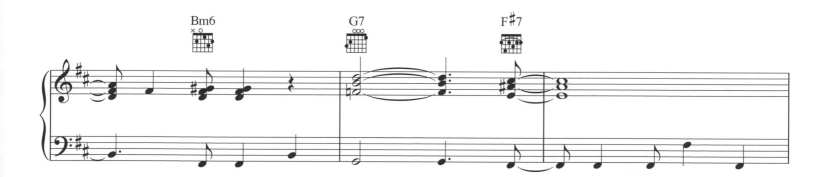

On the double, here come the Neville Brothers.

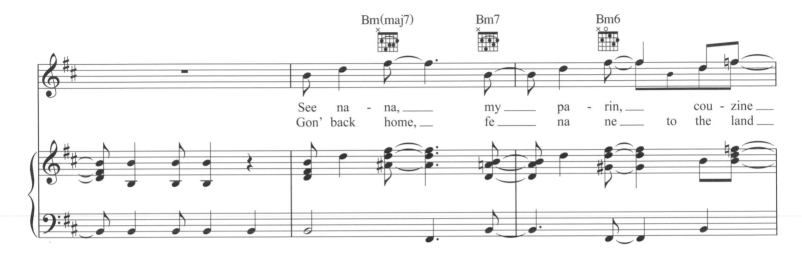

See na - na, _____ my _____ pa - rin, _____ cou - zine _____
Gon' back home, _____ fe _____ na ne _____ to the land _____

_____ and my ma and pa. _____ Gon - na plant _____ my feet _____ on Ram -
_____ of the car - ni - val queen. _____ Well, I'm gon' _____ back home _____ to my _____

To Coda ⊕

- part Street _____ to be there _____ for the Mar - di Gras. _____
_____ ba - by, _____ go - in' back _____ to _____ New _____ Or - leans. _____

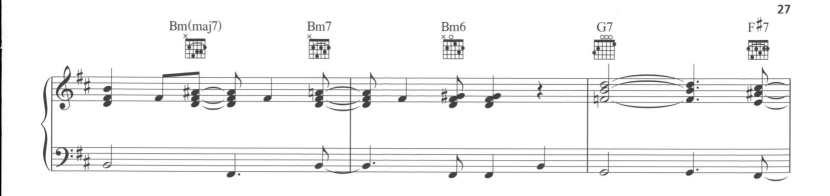

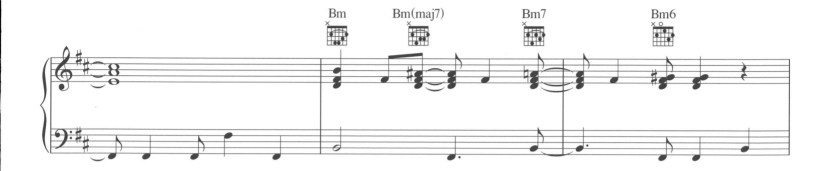

get my fill___ of that e - tou - fee___ 'cause New Or - leans is my home.___

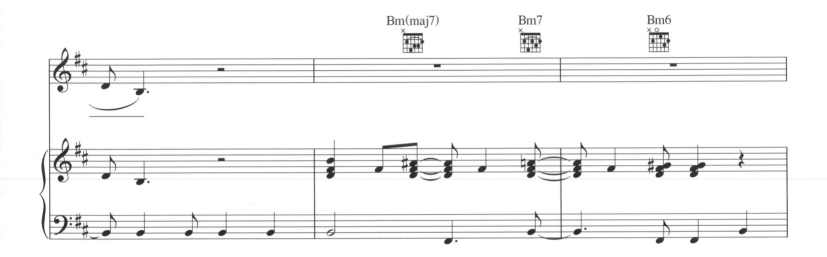

Is that a jumbo jet? No, that's Big Al comin' to put a hurt on you.

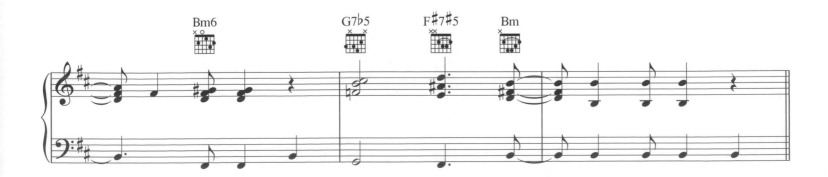

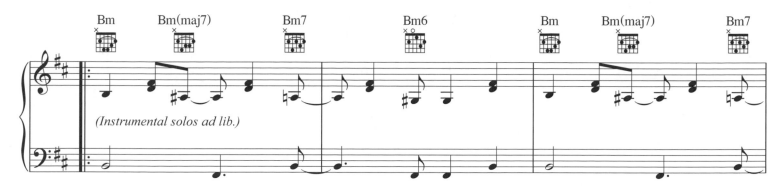

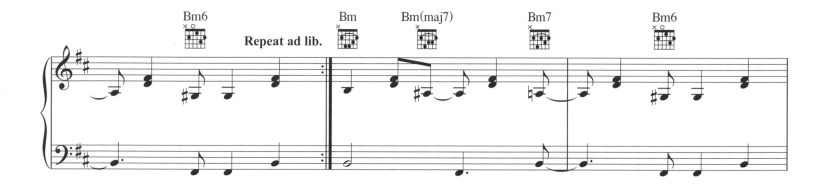

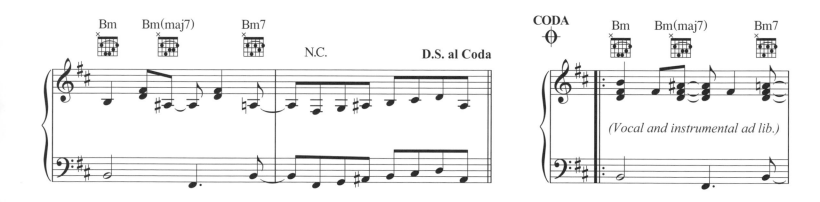

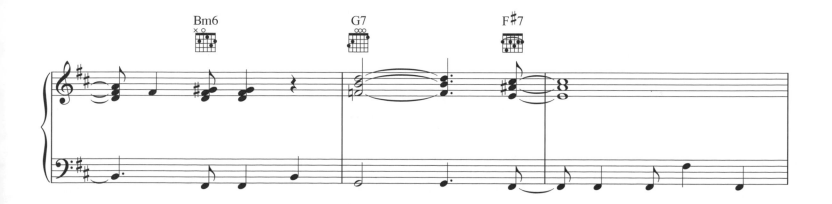

Play 4 times

Gon' back home, ___ fe ___ na ne, ___ to the land ___ of the car - ni - val queen. ___

Well, I'm gon' ____ back home ____ to my ____ ba - by, ____ go - in' back ____

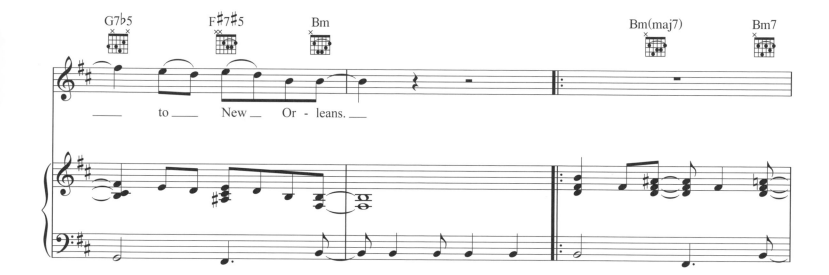

____ to ____ New ____ Or - leans. ____

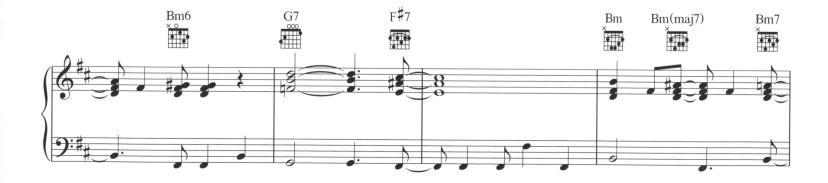

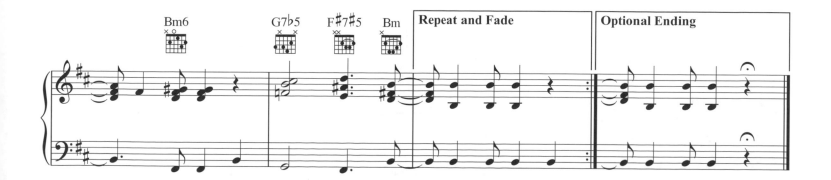

Repeat and Fade

Optional Ending

GRIS-GRIS GUMBO YA YA

Words and Music by
JOHN CREAUX

Moderately slow

They call me Doc-tor John.__ Known as the night trip-per.

Got my satch-el of gris-gris in my hand.__

Day trip-ping up and back down the Bay-

-ou. I'm the last of the best. They call__ me the gris - gris man.

To Coda ⊕

(Spoken): Sell it:

Got man - y cli - ents, call from miles a-

round, run - ning down my _____ pre - scrip - tions.

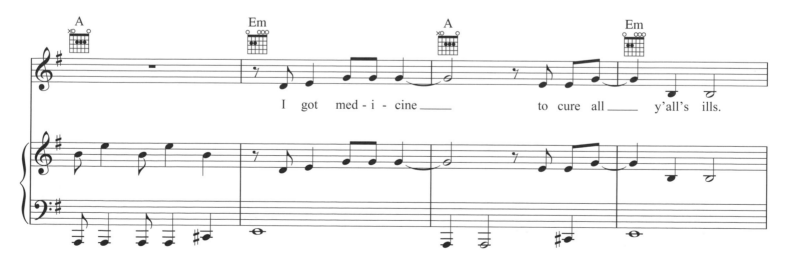

I got med - i - cine _____ to cure all _____ y'all's ills.

I got rem-e-dies of ev-er-y des-crip-tion. No, __

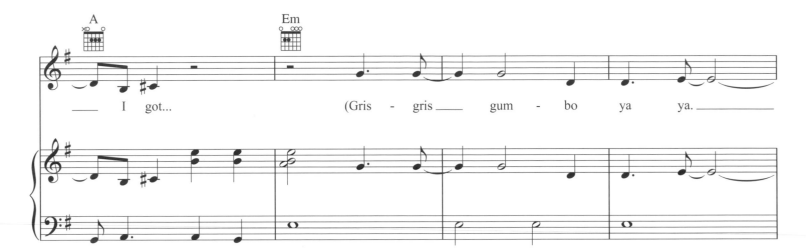

__ I got... (Gris - gris __ gum - bo ya ya. __

__ Hey now, __ bam - ba yeah.) __

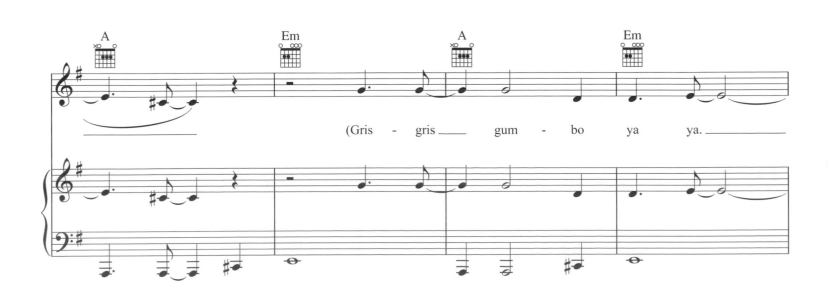

(Gris - gris __ gum - bo ya ya. __

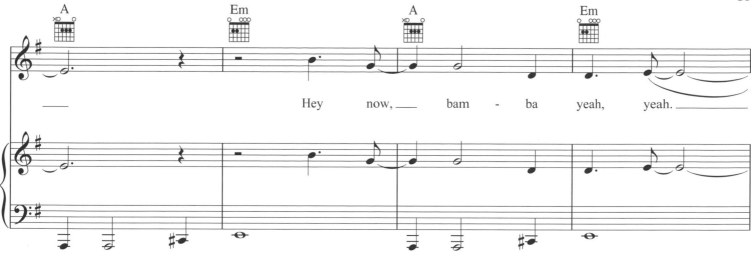

Hey now, ___ bam - ba yeah, yeah. ___

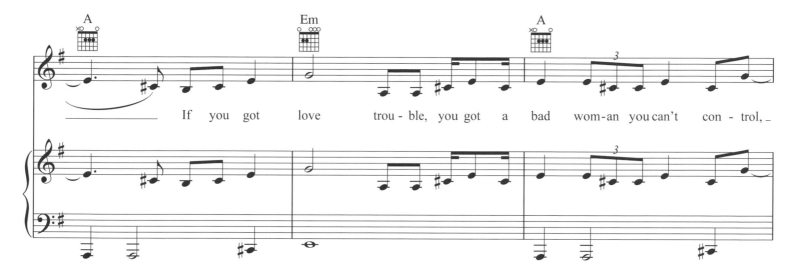

If you got love trou - ble, you got a bad wom-an you can't con - trol, ___

I've got ___ just the thing for you. Some-thing called, "Con - trol and

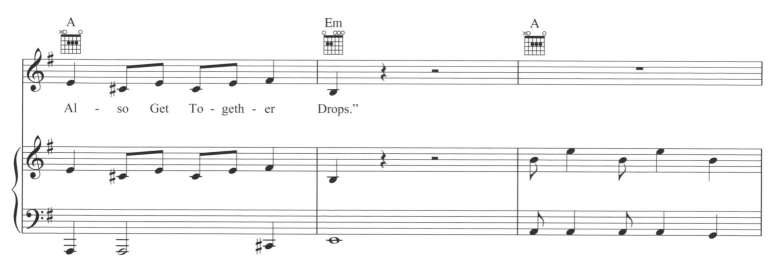

Al - so Get To - geth - er Drops."

If you work too hard _____ and you need a lit-tle rest, try my Eas-y Life

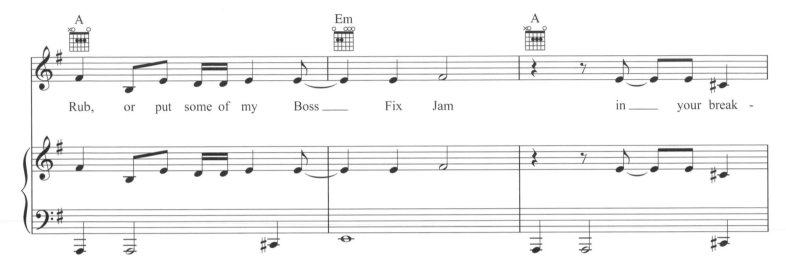

Rub, or put some of my Boss ___ Fix Jam in ___ your break-

fast. Try a lit-tle bit of,... (Gris - gris ___ gum - bo

ya ya. _____ Hey now, ___ bam - ba

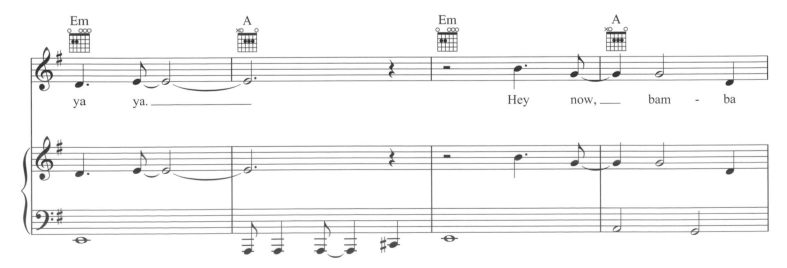

Some warm wa - ter, if your neigh-bors give you trou - ble, put your bus-'ness in the street.

Feel a deuce in my hold ___ card, ___ it just won't ___

___ be beat. Try my Drag - on Blood, ___ my Draw-ing

Pow - der, and my Sleep - er Sand. ___ Have a lit - tle black

yeah. _____ (Gris - gris ___

them un - i - form lov - ers. No, no, _____ no, _____

_____ gum - bo ya ya. _____

_____ no, no, no, no, _____ no, no, _____ no, no, _____

Hey now, _____ bam - ba yeah, yeah.) _____

no, no, _____ yeah, no, _____ no, no, _____ no. Gon' get at it, no, _____

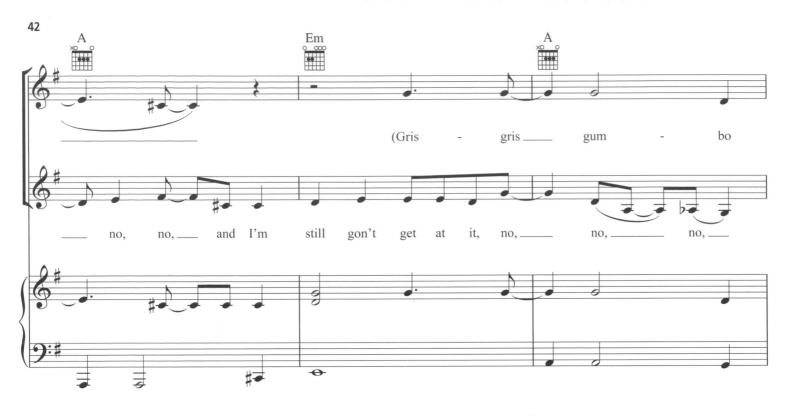

(Gris - gris ___ gum - bo ya ya. ___

Hey now, ___ bam - ba yeah, yeah.) ___

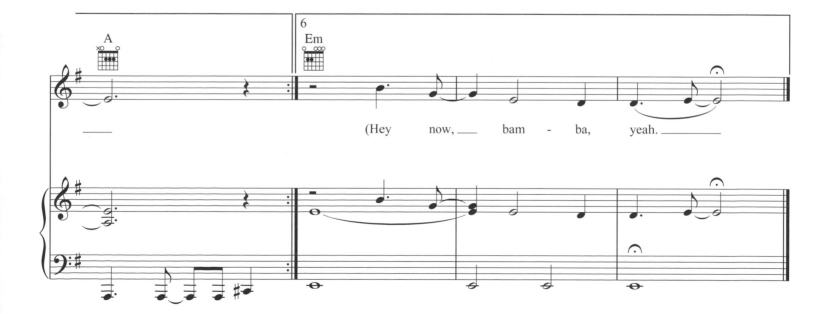

(Hey now, ___ bam - ba, yeah. ___

I WALKED ON GILDED SPLINTERS

Words and Music by
JOHN CREAUX

Moderately, with mystery

Some peo-ple think they jive me but I know they must be cra-zy.

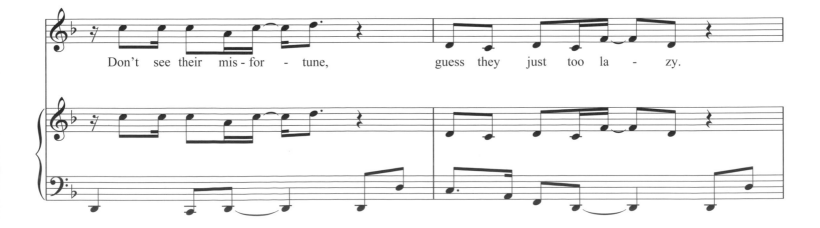

Don't see their mis-for-tune, guess they just too la-zy.

Walk on gild-ed splin-ters with the king___ of the Zu - lu. Dang a man a

kon, kil - ly, kil - ly, kon, kon, walk on gild - ed splin - ters. ___

Ti Al - ber - ta, (ti Al - ber -

- ta, ti Al - ber - ta, ti Al - ber - ta.) I roll out my cof - fin, ___ drink

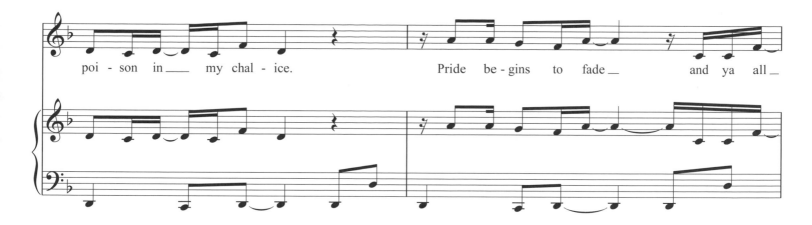

poi - son in ___ my chal - ice. Pride be - gins to fade ___ and ya all ___

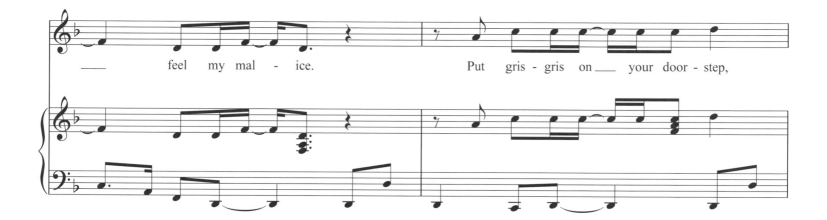

___ feel my mal - ice. Put gris - gris on ___ your door - step,

soon you'll be ___ in the gut - ter. Melt your heart like but - ter a - a - and

I can make ___ you stut - ter. Dang a man a kon, kil - ly, kil - ly, kon, kon,

walk on gild - ed splin - ters. _____ Kon, kil - ly, kil - ly, kon, kon,

walk on gild - ed splin - ters. _____ Kon, kil - ly, kil - ly, kon, kon,

walk on gild - ed splin - ters. _____

Ti Al - ber - ta, (ti Al - ber -

-ta, ti Al-ber - ta, ti Al-ber - ta.) __ Kil - ly, kon, kon, walk on gild-ed splin - ters. __

Kon, kil-ly, kil - ly, kon, kon, walk on gild-ed splin - ters. __ Kon, kil-ly, kil - ly, kon, kon,
(Lead vocal ad lib.)

Play 5 times

walk on gild - ed splin - ters. __

Ti Al - ber - ta, (ti Al - ber - ta, ti Al - ber - ta, ti Al - ber - ta.) __ Land - lord __

__ found me a ta __ na, na, na. Gon', gon' pa di-ab - lo. Ti Al - ber - ta, ti Al - ber - ta, ti Al - ber-

- ta, ti Al - ber - ta. __ Kon, kil-ly, kil - ly, kon, kon, walk on gild - ed splin - ters. __
(Lead vocal ad lib.)

Optional Ending

Repeat and Fade

Kon, kil - ly, kil - ly, kon, kon, walk on gild - ed splin - ters. __

I'M ON A ROLL

Words and Music by MAC REBENNACK
and DOC POMUS

daugh - ter pays me to stay a - way   came to - day ___ too. ___

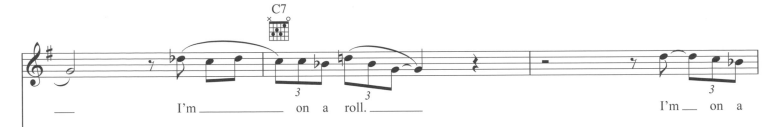

C7

___   I'm _____ on a roll. ___   I'm ___ on a

G7   A7♭9

roll.   I'm ___ on a roll. ___

D9   G   C7   G7   D7

There ain't no con - trol - ling me. ___

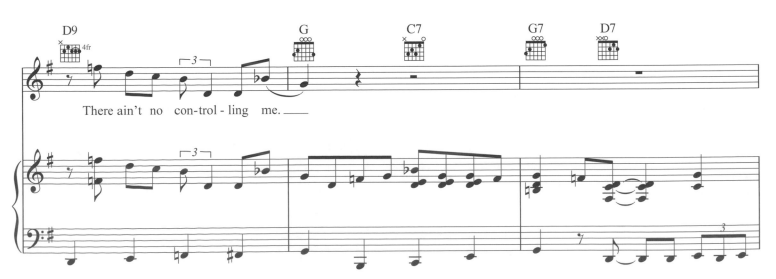

The la-dy who live up-stairs come down to tell me

her hus-band gon-na go a-way for a while.

Now we ain't got-ta sneak a-round no more.

We just sure 'nough live in style. I'm on a

IKO IKO

Words and Music by BARBARA ANN HAWKINS,
JOAN MARIE JOHNSON and ROSA LEE HAWKINS

Moderate Second Line groove

I-ko, I-ko, I-ko, I-ko un-day.

Jock-a-mo fee no ai na-ne, jock-a-mo fee na-ne.

My spy boy told your spy boy, sit-tin' on the Bay-ou. My

spy boy___ told your___ spy boy I'm gon' set___ your tail___ on fire.___ Talk - in' 'bout hey___

___ now, (hey___ now,) hey___ now, (hey___ now,) I - ko, I - ko un - day.

Jock - a - mo fee no ai na - ne,___ jock - a - mo fee na - ne.___

My Ma - rie ___ told your ___ Ma - rie, ___ sitt - in on ___ the Bay - ou. ___
See Ma - rie ___ down the rail - road tracks, ___ I - ko, I - ko, un - day. ___
We gon' down ___ to Bed - ford town, ___ I - ko, I - ko, un - day. ___

My Ma - rie ___ told your ___ Ma - rie ___ gon - na set ___ your flag on fire. ___
Put it here ___ in the chick - en ___ sack ___ wit' your jock - a - mo ___ fee na - ne.
We gon' tell 'em 'bout your mess - in' ___ 'round ___ they gon' jock - a - mo ___ fee na - ne.

We gon' down ___ to Bo - la - sion, ___ I - ko, I - ko un - day. ___
My lil' boy ___ to your lil' boy, ___ get your head ___ on my - o. ___
Both - er what ___ you tell ___ them to, ___ I - ko, I - ko un - day. ___ 'Cause

We gon' catch _ a _ lit-tle ol' sal - mon _ and we're jock-a-mo fee na ne. _ Now, talk - in' 'bout
My lil' girl _ to _ your lil' boy, _ we gon' _ get _ your chick-en _ wire. _ Talk - in' 'bout } hey _
we ain't do _ what _ you tell us to now if you _ jock a - mo fee na ne. _ Now, talk - in' 'bout

_ now, (hey _ now,) hey _ now, (hey _ now,) I - ko, I - ko un - day.

Jock - a - mo fee no ai _ na - ne, _ jock - a - mo fee na - ne. _

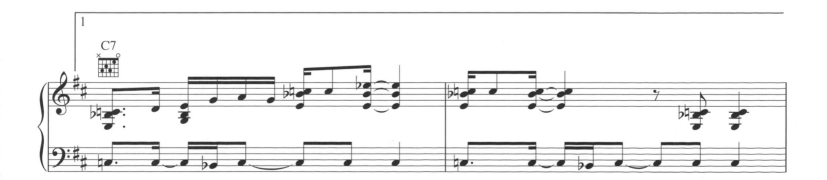

(Lead vocal ad lib.)

Jock-a-mo fee na-nay, — what I say, — un-day.

Jock-a-mo fee na-nay, — what I say, — un-day.

Jock-a-mo fee na-nay, — what I say, — un-day.

Repeat and Fade   **Optional Ending**

I - ko, I - ko un-day,   jock-a-mo fee na-nay. ___
Jock-a-mo fee na-nay, — what I say, — un-day.

JUNKO PARTNER

By ROBERT SHAD

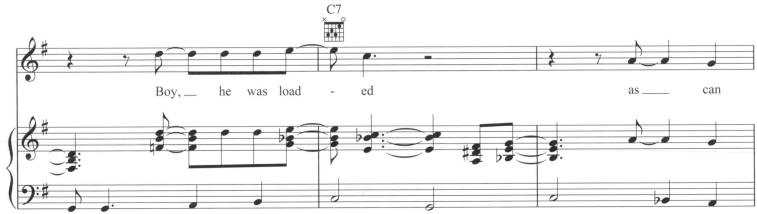

-bled   all o-ver the   street.

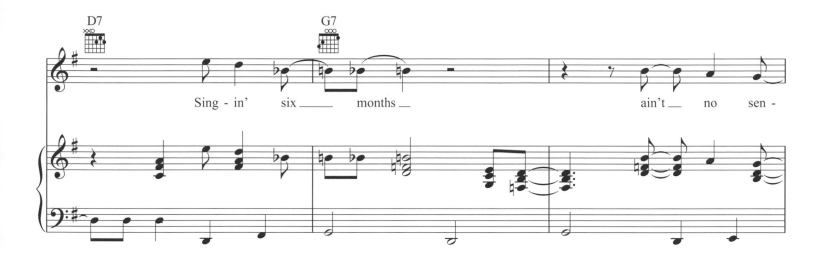

Sing-in' six ____ months ____   ain't ____ no sen-

-tence. ____   Lord, ____ that one ____ year ____

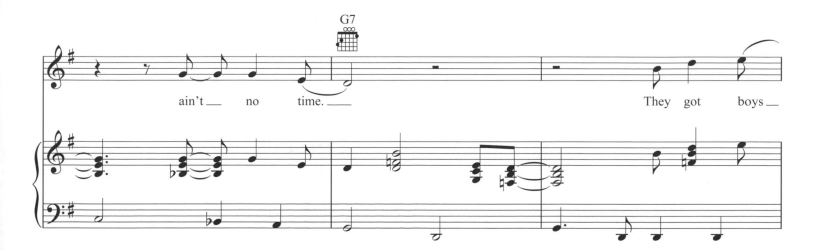

ain't ____ no time. ____   They got boys ____

up on ___ Pon - der - o - sa

serv - in' nine ___ to nine - ty - nine. ___

To Coda ⊕

If I had, ___ if I had, if I

had, a mil - lion dol - lars. Just ___ a one

mil - lion to call my own.

I would buy me the land a - round Par - ish

pri - son and I would grow me

a big mov - ie farm. All right.

CODA

Down the road, down the road, down the road, ___ here ___ he come, ___

___ Mis - ter Jones. _____ Whoo, _____ boy, _____ you're

on your ___ back so ___ hard. ___ Got ___ to say,

Lord - y, Lord. _____ If a pen - ny make a nick - el, a nick - el ___

make a dime. A dime will make you half, a half will make a dol - lar.

Make you hol - ler. Give me whis - key

when I get a lit - tle fris - key. 'Cause it's a my

good drink when you get a lit - tle dry.

Give __ me to-bac - co _____ when I get a lit - tle

sick - ly. _____ But give me her - o - in

be - fore I die. ____ Down the road, down the

road, down the road, down the road, come a Junk-o Part - ner, Part - ner, Part -

(Sax solo on repeat and fade)

ner, Part - ner. Boy, he was load - ed   as   can   be. __

Boy, __ he was __ knocked, knocked, __ knocked, he was   knocked out,   load - ed.

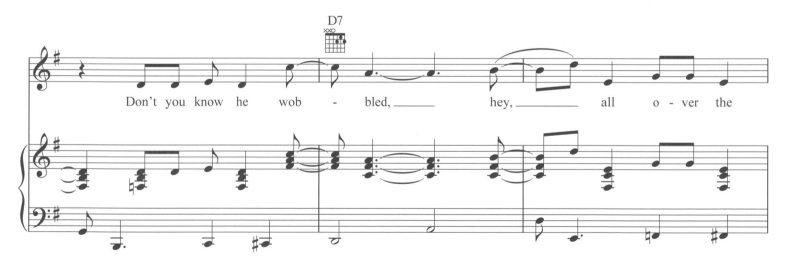

Don't you know he wob - bled, _____   hey, _____   all o - ver the

Optional Ending

Repeat and Fade

street.

MAMA ROUX

Words and Music by
MAC REBENNACK

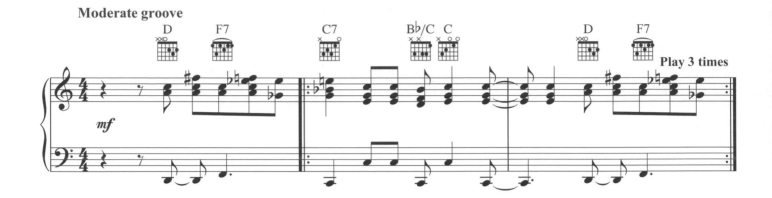

Ma - ma Roux, _____

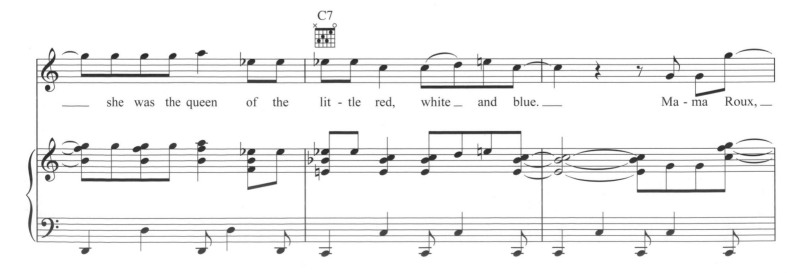

_____ she was the queen of the lit - tle red, white _ and blue. _____ Ma - ma Roux,

she was the queen of the lit-tle red white _ and blue. _

_ Said a, ooh _ why _ can't ya spy _ boy? _ Pre-

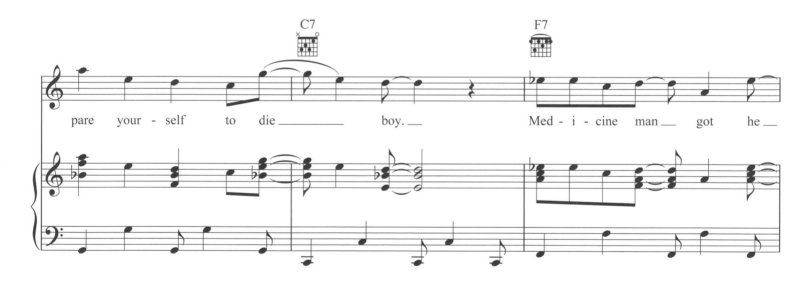

pare your-self to die _____ boy. _ Med-i-cine man _ got he _

_ strong pow-er. You'd know bet-ter than to mess with me. _ Ma-ma Roux, _

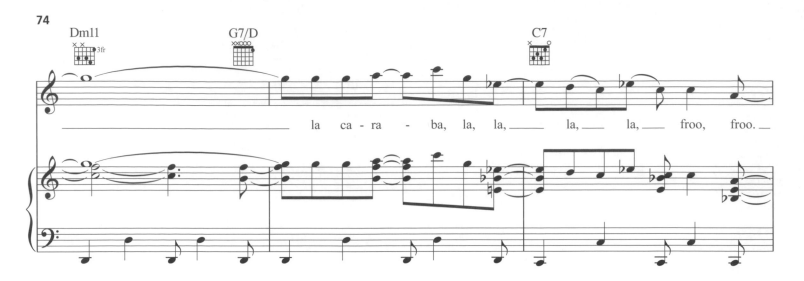

la ca-ra-ba, la, la, la, la, froo, froo.

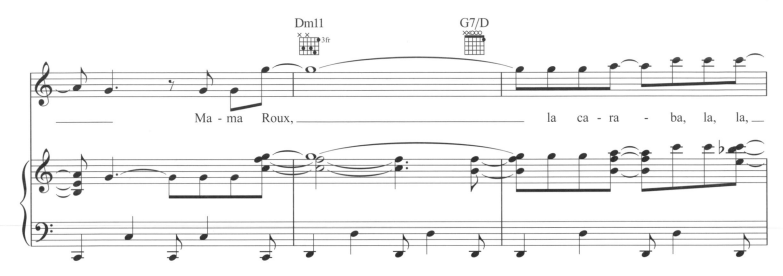

Ma-ma Roux, la ca-ra-ba, la, la,

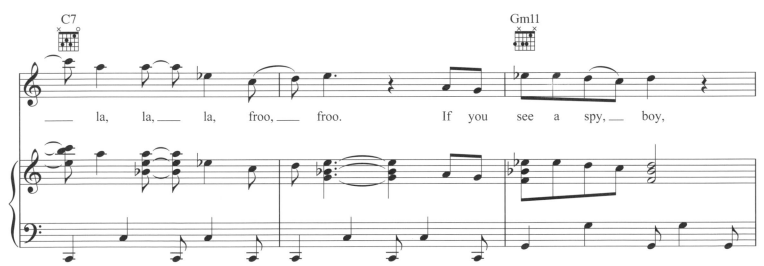

la, la, la, froo, froo. If you see a spy, boy,

sit-tin' in the bush, mess him on the head and give him a push.

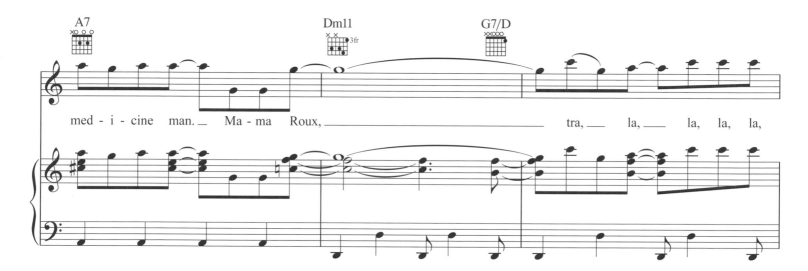

queen is com - in', oom - ba - lay. ___ The queen is com - in' to Hey ___

___ Pock - y Way. ___ You bet - ter not get in the way. ___ Got the

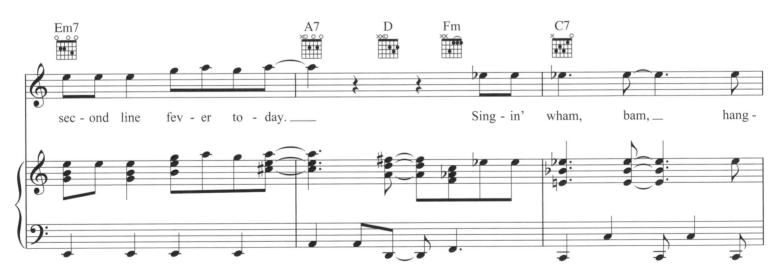

sec - ond line fev - er to - day. ___ Sing - in' wham, bam, ___ hang -

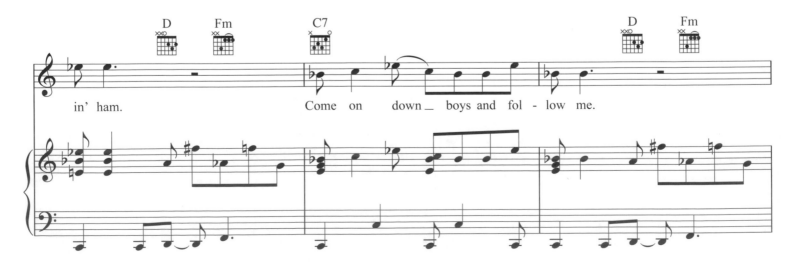

in' ham. Come on down ___ boys and fol - low me.

Wham, bam, __ thank you ma'am. Come on boys __ and fol - low

CODA

D.S. al Coda

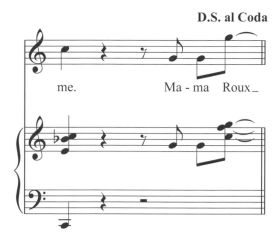

me. Ma - ma Roux __

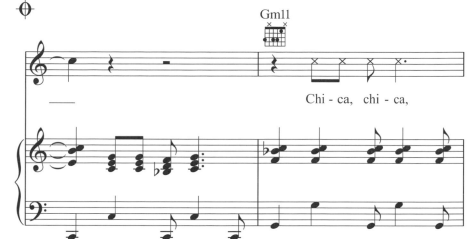

__ Chi - ca, chi - ca,

chi - ca, chi - ca. __ Chi - ca, chi - ca, chi - ca, chi - ca. __

Chi - ca, chi - ca, chi - ca, chi - ca. __ Chi - ca, chi - ca,

chi - ca, chi - ca. _____   Wham, bam, _____   thank

you ma'am.   Come on boys_ now and fol - low me.

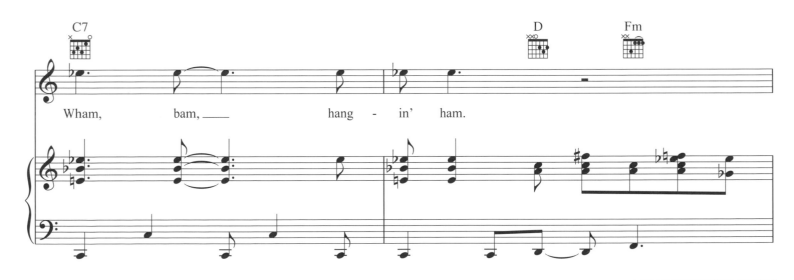

Wham, bam, _____   hang - in' ham.

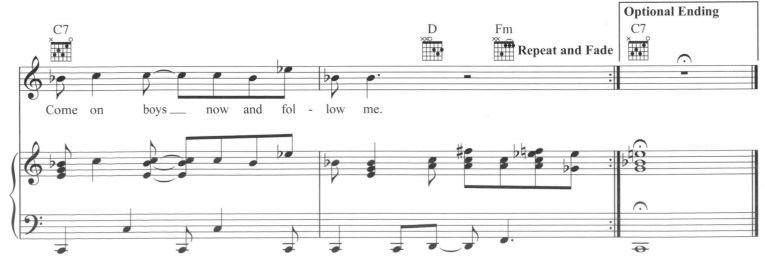

Come on boys_ now and fol - low me.

RIGHT PLACE, WRONG TIME

Words and Music by
MAC REBENNACK

Moderate Funk groove

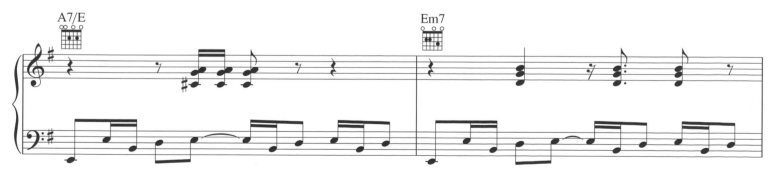

* Recorded a half step lower.

I been in the right place ___ but it must have been the

wrong time. ___ I'd have said the right thing ___ but I must have used the

wrong line. ___ I been in the right trip ___ but I must have used the

wrong car. ___ Head was in a bad place ___ and I won-der what it's

good for. ___ I been in the right place but it must have been the

wrong time. ___ My head was in a bad place ___ but I'm hav-in' such a

good time. I've been runn-in' try'n to get hung

up in my mind, _____ ooh. Just got to give my-self a good

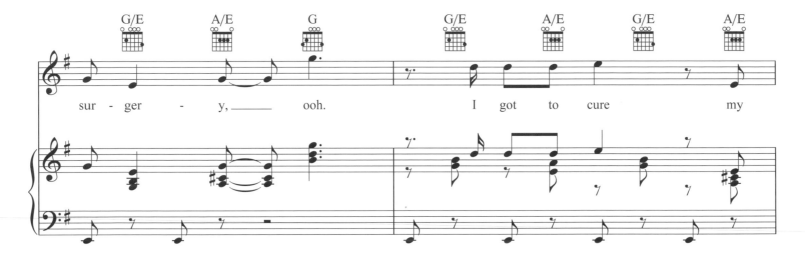

wrong song. __ I been in the right vein __ but it seems like the
wrong line. __ I'd have took the right road __ but I must have took a

To Coda ⊕

wrong arm. __ 'Cause I been in the right world but it seems like the
wrong turn. __ I'd have took a right move but I made it at the

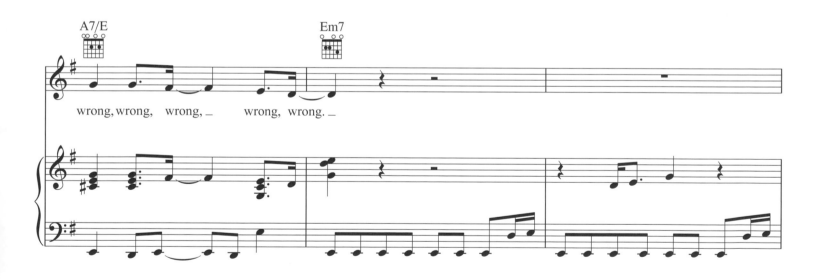

wrong, wrong, wrong, __ wrong, wrong. __

Slip - pin', dodg - in', sneak - in', peep - in', hid - in' out down the street, ooh.

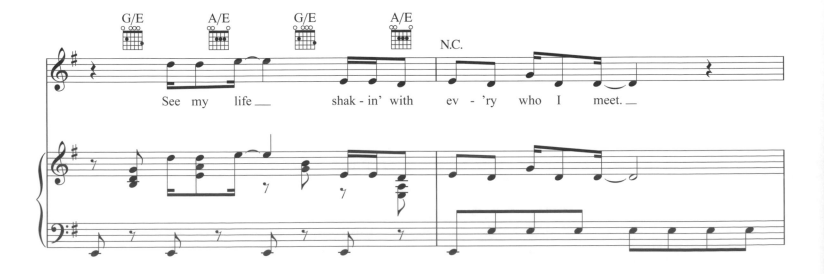

See my life __ shak - in' with ev - 'ry who I meet. __

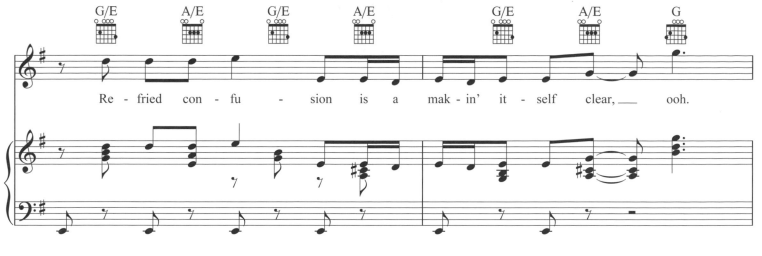

Re - fried con - fu - sion is a mak - in' it - self clear, ___ ooh.

Won - der which way do I go to get on out of here? 'Cause I was in the

D.S. al Coda

N.C.

CODA

Repeat and Fade

wrong time. ___   I went on the right trip   but I made it in the
good place   and I won - der what it's
(Ad lib. lyrics after repeat.)

Optional Ending

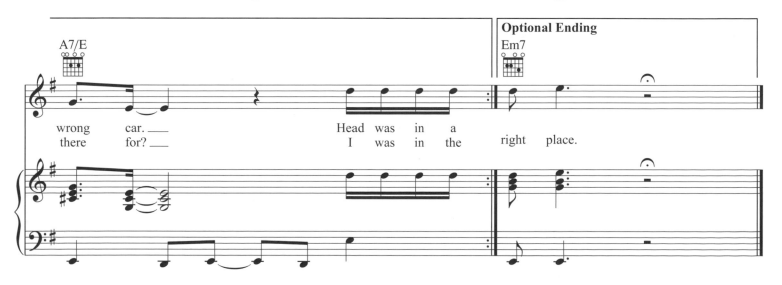

wrong car. ___   Head was in a   right place.
there for? ___   I was in the

MY KEY DON'T FIT
(Somebody Changed The Lock)

Words and Music by
MAC REBENNACK

front porch all night long, _____ and I, 'n I

know _____ some-thing is def - i - nite - ly go - ing on _____ wrong. _____

_____ You know that the

lights is dim, _____ the shades are way down low. _____

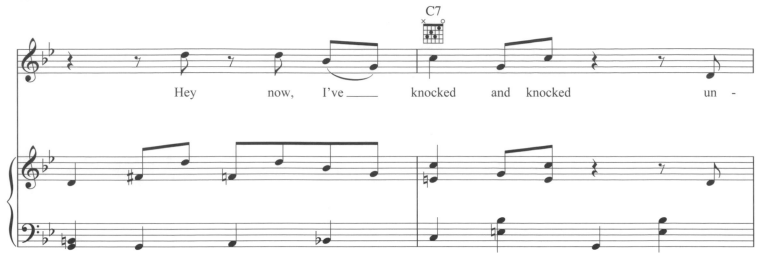

Hey now, I've _____ knocked and knocked un -

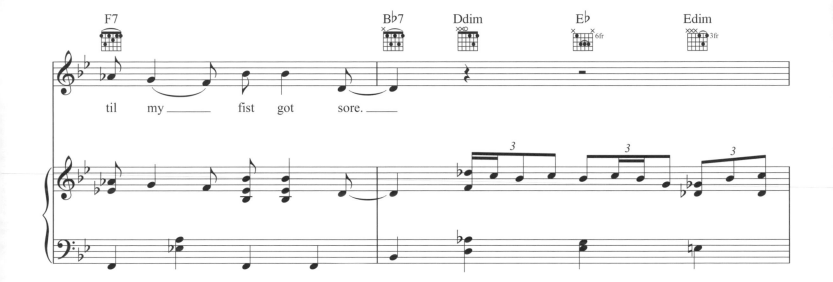

til my _____ fist got sore. _____

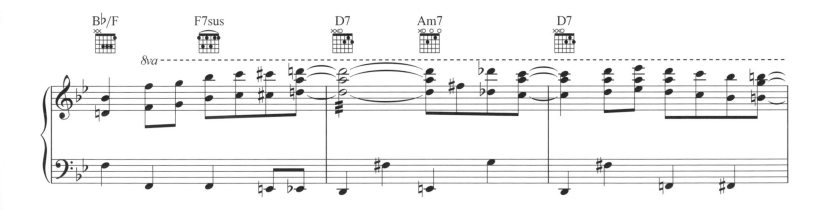

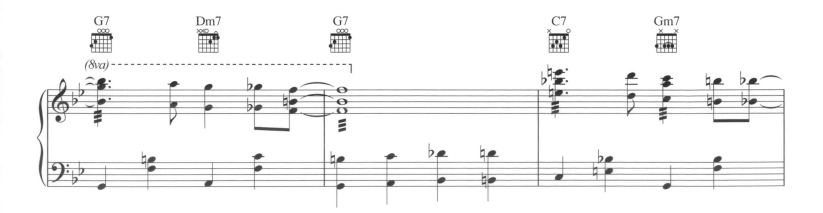

I've been stand-

-ing on my front porch all night long, __

__ yeah, __ now, and I know __ some-thing is def-

i-nite-ly go-ing on wrong. __

Yeah ___ now, ___ now, I know you changed ___ the lock ___

___ on my door. ___ Yeah, lord, ___ my

key, it won't ___ fit in my lock no more, ___

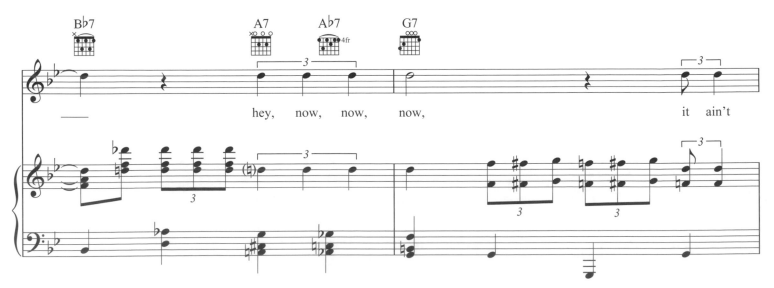

___ hey, now, now, now, it ain't

turned the lock, 'cause me and my ___ wom-an is no more. ___

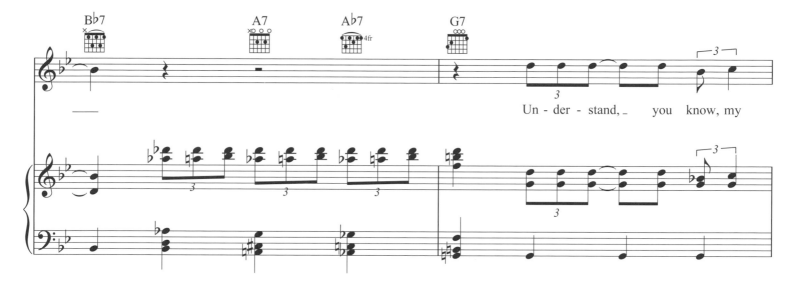

___ Un-der-stand, ___ you know, my

key it won't a - fit in that lock no more.

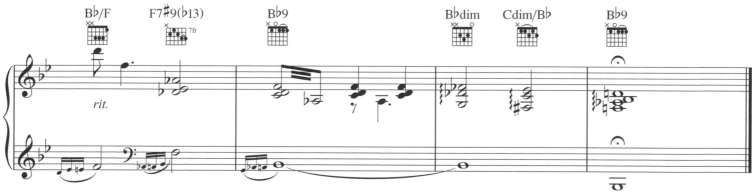

QUALIFIED

Words and Music by MAC REBENNACK
and JESSIE HILL

(Spoken:) *Looky here.*

Uh huh, check it out.

Looky here, looky here.

Your steak ___ ain't no hip-per than my pork chop. ___

Your Cad - il - lac ___ ain't no hip-per than my bus ___

___ stop. ___ Your cham - pagne ___

ain't no hip - per than my so - da pop. ___

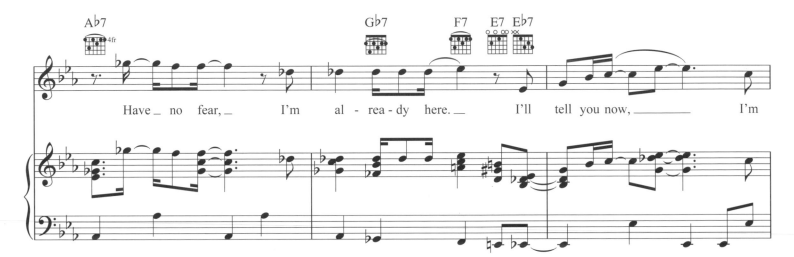

Your top __ hat __ ain't no bad-der than __ my gin - ger brim. __
so - cial __ life __ ain't no bet - ter than __ my hot __ dog stand. __

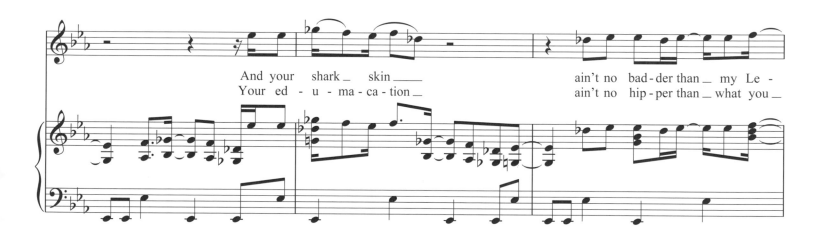

And your shark __ skin _____ ain't no bad-der than __ my Le -
Your ed - u - ma - ca - tion __ ain't no hip - per than __ what you __

- vi's, Jim. _____ The mon - ey you got,
___ un - der - stand. __ Your wom - an that you got,

it ain't no bad-der than a high-er spend-in' Bens. ___
she ain't no hip-per than a how ___ lov - in' been. ___

All I've got's a lit-tle bit of
I've got the pow - er ___

com - mon sense. ___ I be-lieve in my heart the best e. d. is ex -
to con - trol. ___ I can see clear ___ through your

per - i - ence. ___ }
blind - fold. ___ } And I wan-na tell you now, ___ I'm

qual - i - fied. __ You know __ that I'm qual - i - fied. _____ Don't you know that I'm

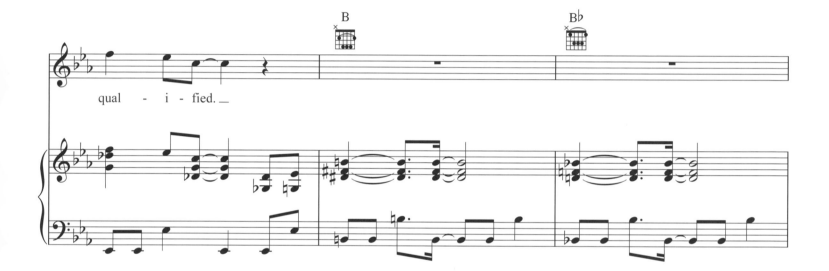

qual - i - fied. __

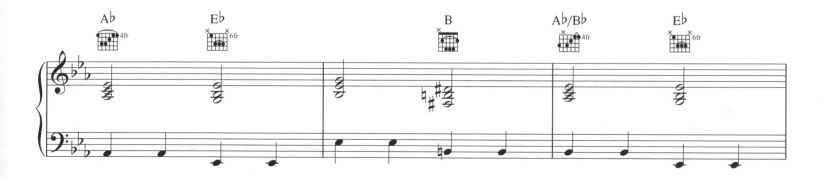

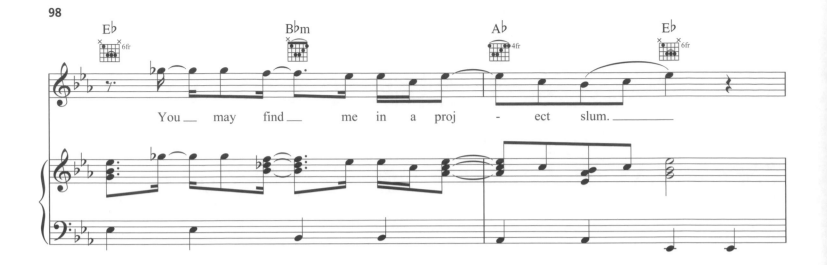

You __ may find __ me in a proj - ect slum. _____

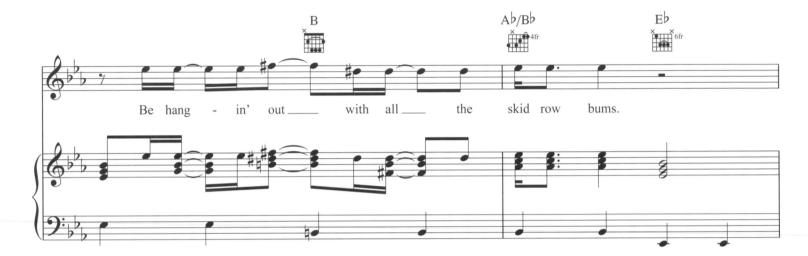

Be hang - in' out _____ with all ___ the skid row bums.

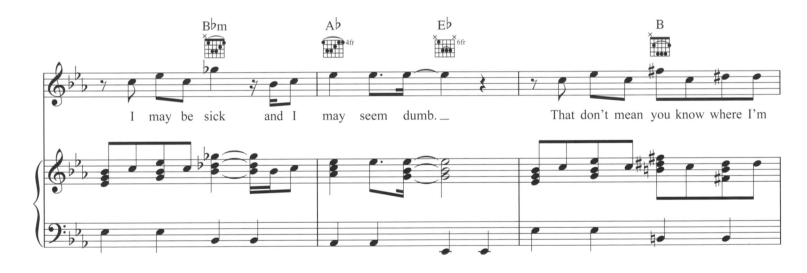

I may be sick and I may seem dumb. __ That don't mean you know where I'm

com - in' from. __

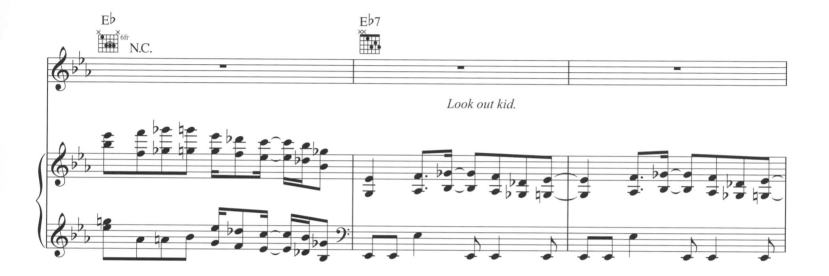

Look out kid.

Just make a little room, uh.   Your

D.S. al Coda

CODA

Ad lib. vocals and instrumental

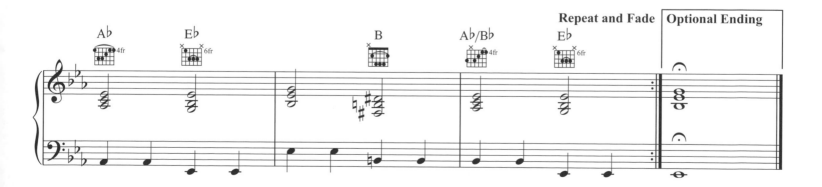

Repeat and Fade | **Optional Ending**

SUCH A NIGHT

Words and Music by
MAC REBENNACK

you let me know ___ that this was my chance. ___

Well, you came ___ there with my best friend, Jim, ___ and here I ___ am ___ try-ing to

steal you a-way from him. Oh, ___ but if I don't do it, you know some-

bod-y else will. ___ If I don't do it, you know some-bod-y else will. ___ If

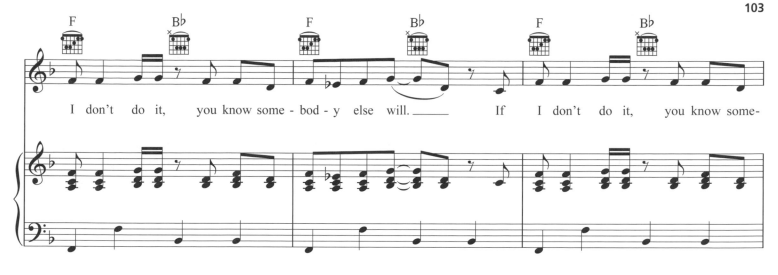

I don't do it, you know some-bod-y else will. _____ If I don't do it, you know some-

D.S. al Coda

bod-y else will. _____ And it's

CODA

_____

Yeah, I could-n't be-lieve my ear; _____ and my

heart just _ skipped a beat; then you told _ me to take you _

walk-ing down the street. Oh yeah, you came ___ here with my

best friend, Jim, ___ and here I ___ am, ___ I'm steal-ing you a - way from him.

Oh, ___ but if I don't do it, you know some-bod-y else will. ___ If

I don't do it, you know some-bod-y else will. ___ If I don't do it, you know some-

bod-y else will. _____ If I don't do it, you know some-bod-y else will, _ 'cause it's

such a night.
(Vocals 1st time only)

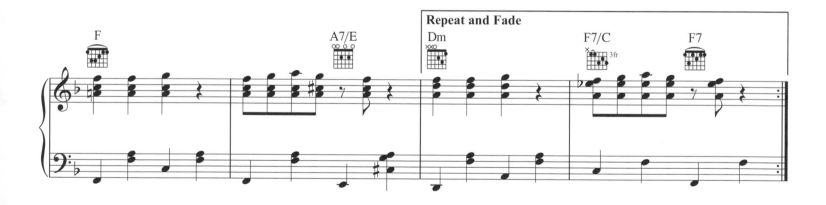

Repeat and Fade

Optional Ending

TIPITINA

By HENRY ROELAND BYRD

Tip - i - ti - na, _____ tra - la - la - la.

Piano solo ad lib.

Tip - i - ti - na, -a, -a, -a, _____ tra - la - la. _____

Tip - i - ti - na, ooh, ___ la mal -

-la, wal - la, won't you tra - la, _____ 'Ti - na, -na.

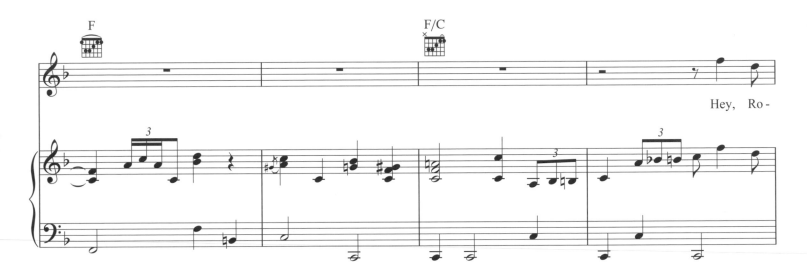

Hey, Ro-

ber - ta,   oh, Ro - ber - ta,   can you hear

me _____ call - ing you? _____   You are

three times ___ sev - en, ba - by, and you know what you ___ want to

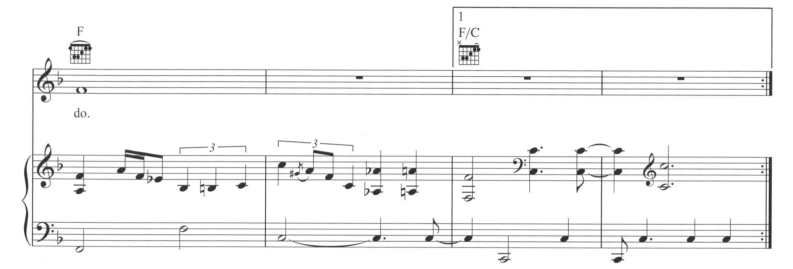

do.

(Solo ends) Hey now, boy, ___ we go - ing

down on ___ the gal - low, and we sure ___

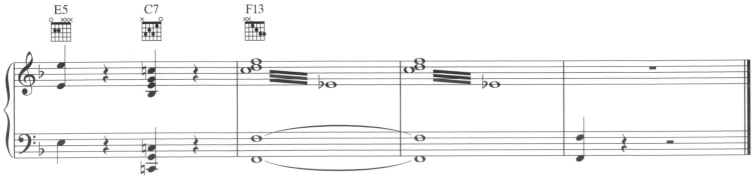

YOUR AVERAGE KIND OF GUY

Words and Music by MAC REBENNACK
and DOC POMUS

Moderately, in 4

I'm o - ver - worked, un - der - paid, __ un - der - loved, _____ and o - ver - laid. __ Oh __ me, __ oh __ me, oh __ my, __ I'm _____ your

*Recorded a half step lower.

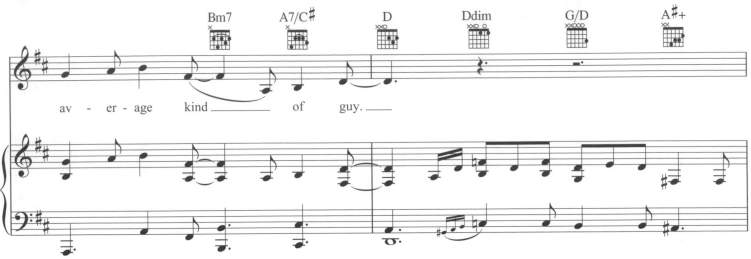

av- er- age kind _____ of guy. ____

Hate my job, _____ and I hate _ my wife, _

I hate my house, and I hate my _ life.

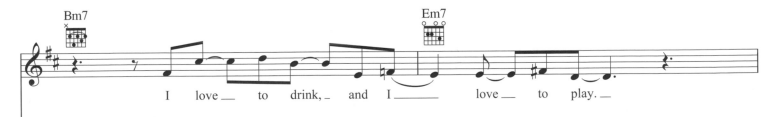

I love _ to drink, _ and I _____ love _ to play. ___

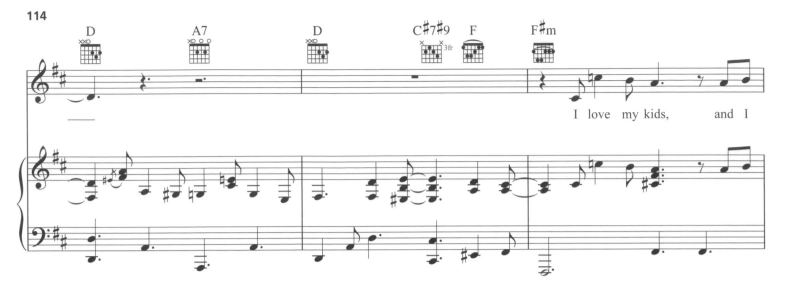

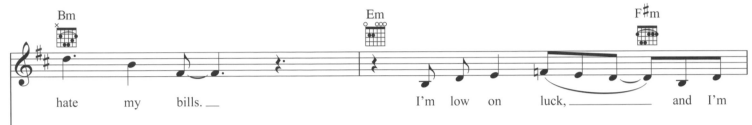

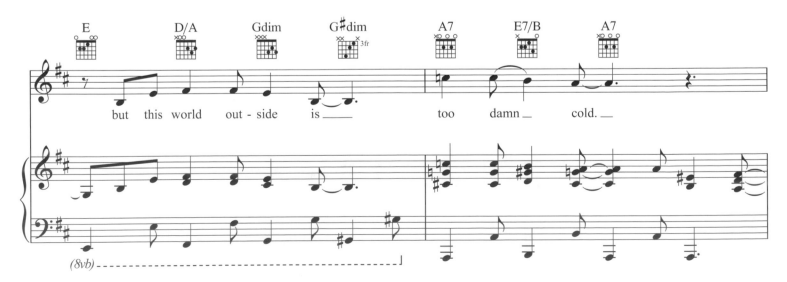

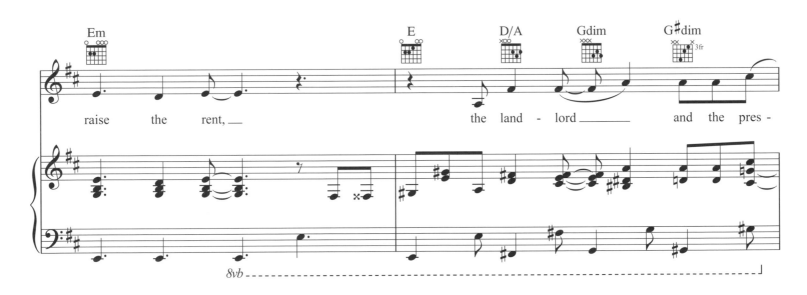

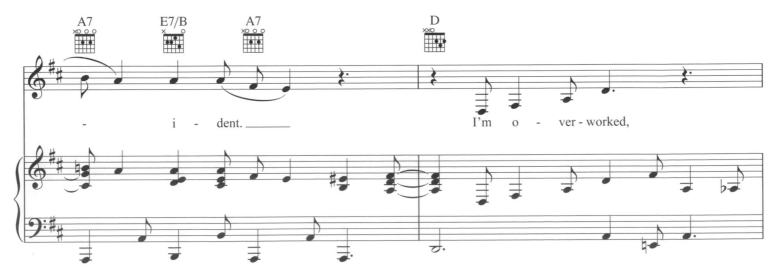

un - der - paid, ___ un - der - loved, _____ and

o - ver - laid. ___ Oh _____ me, _____ oh _____

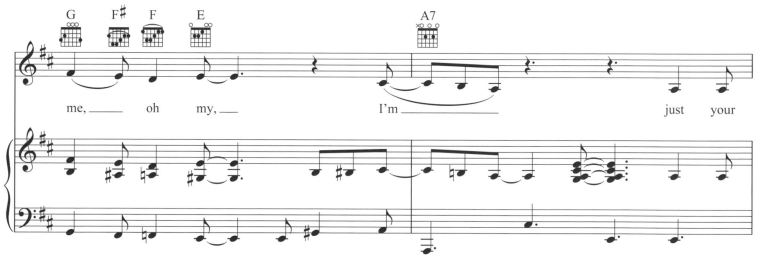

me, _____ oh my, ___ I'm _____ just your

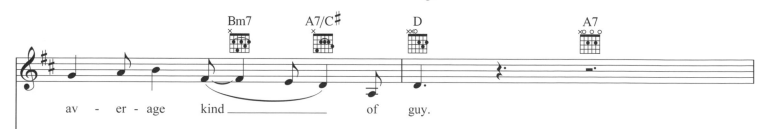

av - er - age kind _____ of guy.

ZU-ZU MAMOU

Words and Music by
MAC REBENNACK

my com-mand._ I'm a zu-zu man._ I got a

bag of mag-ic in both of my hands. I'm a zu-zu man._

When your prob-lems get out__ of hand,__ see the zu-zu man._

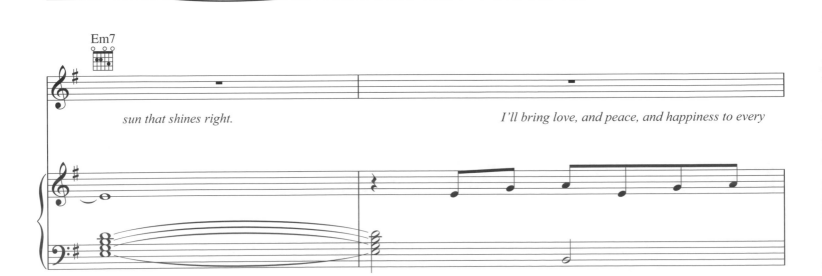

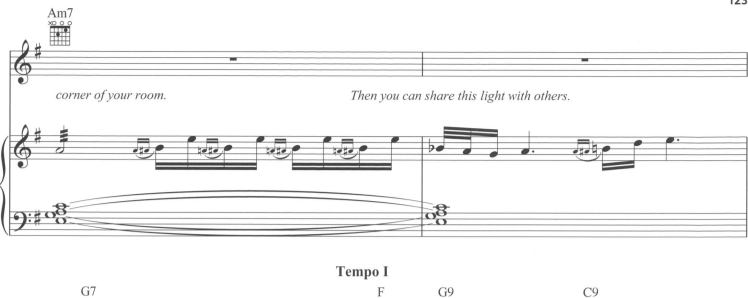

corner of your room.   *Then you can share this light with others.*

Tempo I

Peace, sisters and brothers.   This is what we

all should do (oh,   live and die,...).   Peo - ple live and die.

Here's some good ad - vice:

Be sweet, and be mer - ry,   nev - er, ev - er con - trar -

Am

\- y.   I got a bag___ of mag - ic in both of my hands.___ I'm a

Em7   **Am**

zu - zu man.___   And that ter - ri - ble speak,

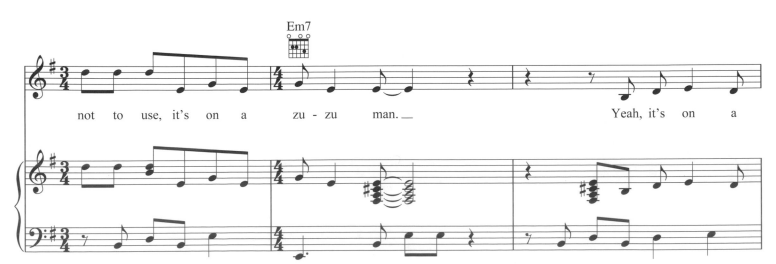

Em7

not to use, it's on a zu - zu man.___   Yeah, it's on a

zu - zu man. And I dig. *Lead vocal ad lib. to end (See additional lyrics)*

Optional Ending

Repeat and fade

Additional Lyrics (ad lib.)

Spoken: I'd pigtail.
Love tell the tale.
That's all the diff'rence.
Call me. Call again. That's right, baby,
Yessir. Yeah, I've seen you better than tonight.
Now why's he gone down to Belville?
That's two recorded.
Now, menfolk,... The gang, they'll never catch him,
'Cause he ain't doing nothing, and it's outta sight.